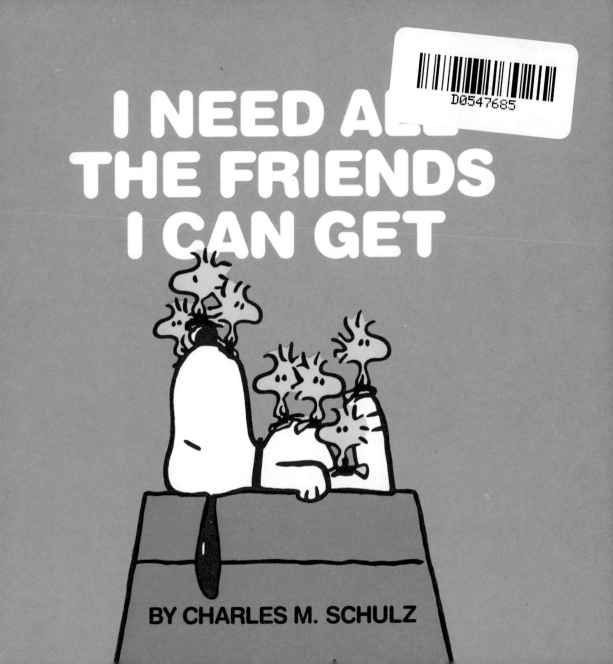

I NEED ALL THE FRIENDS I CAN GET

BY CHARLES M. SCHULZ

First published in this edition 1982
Published by William Collins Sons and Co Ltd, London and Glasgow
Copyright © 1981 by United Feature Syndicate, Inc.
All rights reserved.
Based on "I Need All the Friends I Can Get"
by Charles M. Schulz
Copyright © 1964 by United Feature Syndicate, Inc.
Printed in the United Kingdom by William Collins Sons and Co. Ltd.
ISBN 0 00 195323 0

Charles M. Schulz, creator of Snoopy and the
PEANUTS® gang is world famous. His humour
is unique...its appeal universal.

The first edition of I NEED ALL THE FRIENDS
I CAN GET appeared in 1964 and was an
immediate best seller. This new enlarged
version all in colour contains three times as
many pages, with new drawings, new
sentiments, new fun — new friendship.

Other books by Charles M. Schulz in this new
enlarged format are: HAPPINESS IS A WARM
PUPPY, LOVE IS WALKING HAND-IN-HAND
and CHRISTMAS IS TOGETHER TIME.

A friend is someone who laughs at all your jokes.

A friend is someone who'll do your homework while you watch TV.

A friend is someone who'll speak up for you.

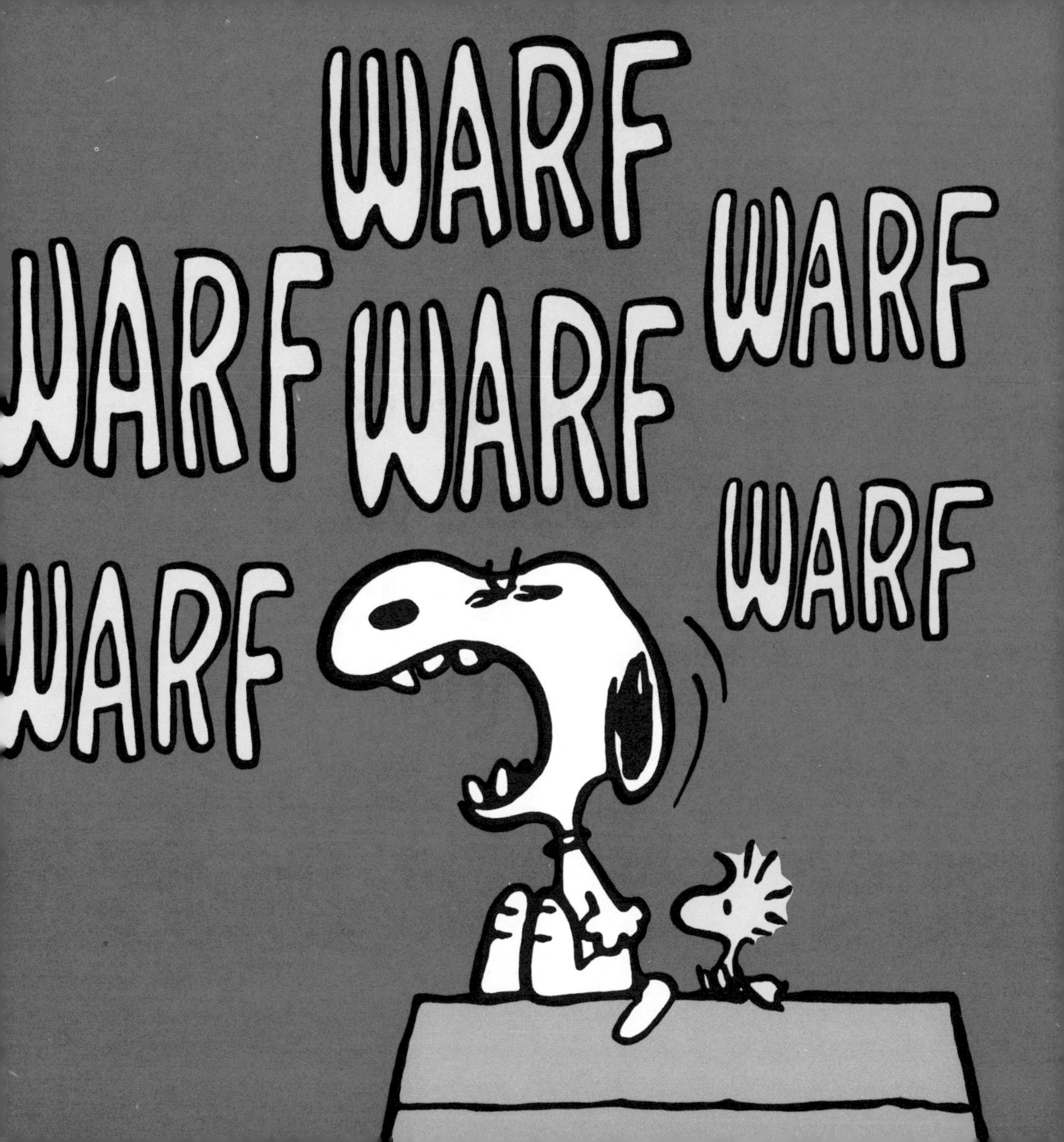
WARF
WARF
WARF
WARF
WARF
WARF

A friend is someone who understands sharing.

A friend is someone who answers your letters.

A friend is someone who makes you feel comfortable and relaxed.

**A friend is
someone who attracts
the teacher's attention
when you don't want her
to call on you.**

A friend is someone who says your winning goal wasn't "just a lucky shot."

A friend is someone you can depend on even when it's not "fair weather."

A friend is someone who remembers you on Valentine's Day.

A friend is
someone who
thinks about
marshmallow sundaes
at midnight...
just like you do.

A friend is someone who makes you laugh when you're hurting.

A friend is someone who thinks you're a good dancer.

A friend is someone who doesn't get you involved unless you want to be.

A friend is someone who eats lunch with you on your first day at a new school.

A friend is
someone who
leaves you alone
while you're watching
the "soaps."

A friend is someone who asks to see your vacation pictures.

A friend is someone who'll do anything to cheer you up.

A friend is
someone who
likes you as much
as he likes
his piano.

A friend is someone who'll massage your back.

A friend is someone who doesn't mind if you cry.

A friend is someone you can call on in an emergency.

A friend is someone who doesn't bug you about every little mistake.

A friend is someone who doesn't try to shoot you down.

A friend is someone who has respect for your possessions.

A friend is someone who doesn't invite you to his piano recital.

A friend is someone who likes the same TV programs you do.

A friend is someone who'll take care of you when you have the vapors.

A friend is someone who adds meaning to your life.

A friend is someone who doesn't gossip about you.

A friend is someone who sticks with your team...rain or shine.

A friend is someone who remembers to bring the can of balls.

A friend is someone who'll give you a free ride.

A friend is
someone who
tells you not to worry
if you double-fault
and lose the
winning point.

A friend is someone who appreciates your kind of music.

A friend is someone you can telephone after midnight.

A friend is someone who'll go jogging with you at six in the morning.

A friend is someone who'll let you sulk if you feel like it.

A friend is someone who'll try to find you when you're lost.

A friend is someone who respects you even though you're not as big.

A friend is someone who doesn't talk about your braces.

A friend is someone you can kiss on the nose.

A friend is someone who doesn't move in on your territory.

A friend is someone who doesn't laugh at you.

A friend is someone who knows when to keep quiet.

A friend is someone who doesn't tell you anything "for your own good."

A friend is someone you can trust.

A friend is
someone who
gets a lower grade
than yours and keeps
you from being
the dumbest
in the class.

A friend is someone who doesn't play rough.

A friend is someone who rescues you when you get yourself into a stupid situation.

CHOP
CHOP
CHOP
CHOP
CHOP

A friend is someone who gives you the hard cover edition instead of waiting for the paperback to come out.

A friend is someone who doesn't make fun of you even when you do dumb things.

A friend is someone who'll pick you up when you're down.

A friend is someone who helps you forget your self-doubts.

A friend is someone who offers to bring the dessert to your dinner party.

A friend is someone who puts you up for membership in his club.

A friend is someone who says "My treat."

A friend is someone who doesn't criticize your personal philosophy even if it's wishy-washy.

A friend is someone who doesn't intrude on your solitude.

A friend is someone you can count on.